RISING STAR

Maths

Written by Akanksha Arora
Edited by Priyanka Dey
Illustrated by Neeraj S. Roy
Designed by Nirbhay Kumar

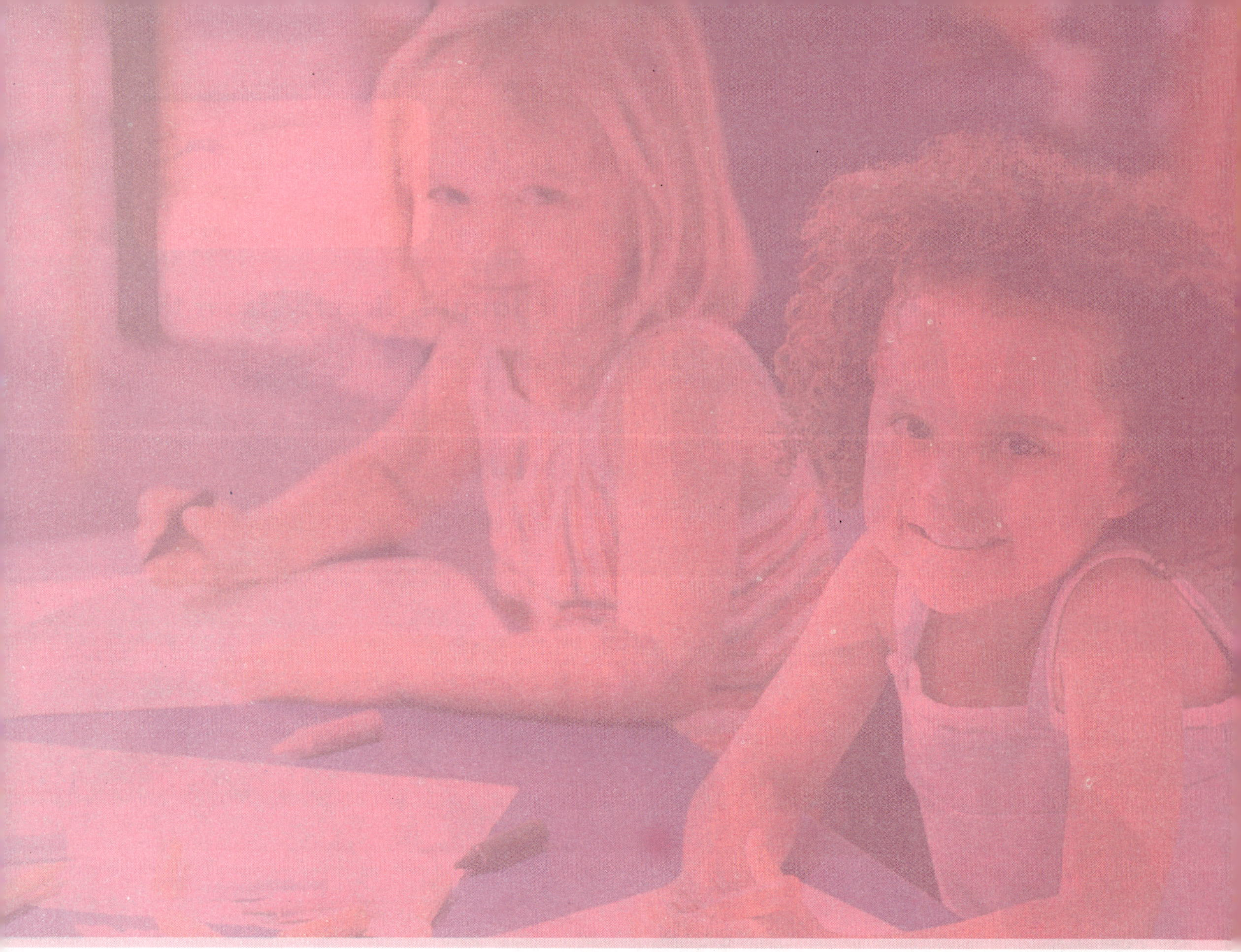

Acknowledgement: Manmeet Narang

www.pegasusforkids.com

Published by Kuldeep Jain for B. JAIN PUBLISHERS (P) Ltd., D-157, Sector 63, Noida - 201307, U.P

Printed in India

PREFACE

Mathematics is abstract in nature. If taught directly from the textbook, children may find it difficult to understand and develop a fear forever. Hence, it is crucial to show children how it exists in their environment. Using concrete experiences by giving material to count and observe in their surroundings, they see it as a part of their life. The book introduces concepts through contexts with two characters, Lizi and Ben. The contexts help children see the purpose of studying various mathematical concepts and how they are used in daily life. The early development of number concepts is critical to develop a positive attitude about mathematics. Special methods and activities involving concrete material help students develop numeracy skills.

Students are introduced to **Pre-number concepts** like 'Big', 'Small', 'Tall', and 'Short'. Comparing sizes helps develop skills of estimation and measurement. Concepts such as 'Heavy' and 'Light' help them identify the difference in the weight of objects by looking at their sharp observable differences.

Positional vocabulary is introduced, such as 'Near', 'Far', 'In', 'Out', 'Up' and 'Down'. This understanding lays the foundation for students to develop the sense of direction, distance and location. It is used in reading maps and graphs in higher grades.

Some other concepts introduced in the book are:

Matching—It helps students notice how things are alike or different.

Sorting—It is an essential pre-number skill, which helps children form groups on the basis of a criterion, such as colour, shape and size.

One to one correspondence—It is the ability to match an object of one set with an object of another set. This later helps in comparing quantities.

Before learning to arrange numbers in a sequence, students need to learn to put things in a sequence. **Seriation** is the ordering of objects by size.

Children develop number sense of **Numbers** ranging from 1 to 10. This means to understand quantification (sense of quantity), representation, and relationship between numbers. They can connect the number and numerals to the quantities they represent using concrete material. They also learn to write the numbers.

Children learn subitizing, i.e. instant recognition of a number pattern without counting. **Patterns** can be seen in things, floor designs, clothes and paper materials. Children start recognizing patterns at a very young age, which enhances their observation skills. They also develop the sense of time by looking at the activities in the order of their occurrence. They start sequencing various activities of their day. Through data collection, they learn to collect data and derive information from it.

CONTENTS

Matching 7

Sorting 10

Pairing 13

One-to-One Correspondence 16

Big and Small 19

Sequencing 24

Numbers 27

Inside and Outside 92

Near and Far 96

Subitizing 100

Shapes 103

Patterns 116

Heavy and Light 120

Long and Short 123

Time 127

Up and Down 131

Data Collection 135

Matching

Hey! I am Lizi. I am going for a swim with my friend, Mini. We have got similar (matching) things. Have a look!

Lizi

Mini

Mini wants the same things as Lizi. Draw a line to match the things.

Lizi has her own set of things, and Mini wants the same things. Draw a line to match the things.

Sorting

Naughty Ben has put some things in the wrong jars. Find the odd thing in each jar and cross it out.

Find the odd one out in each set of objects.

Ben went to his uncle's shop. While running around in the shop, he dropped some things from the shelves. He picked those things up and arranged them, but they got mixed up. Cross the things that do not belong where he placed them.

Pairing

Look at Lizi's house. It is so clean. She has arranged different things in pairs. Observe how she has paired the things.

Things that go together should be paired. Draw a line to form pairs.

Here are some more things that go together. Draw a line to form pairs.

One-to-One Correspondence

The butterflies in the garden were looking for flowers. Look, each one has found a flower. Trace the dots to help them reach the flowers.

Here are some photos and photo frames. Match one photo to one photo frame.

Note: Children match objects one-to-one and later this equips them to compare two sets of objects to identify more and less.

Lizi and her friends have brought juice packs for their family members. Draw one straw each for the number of juice packs shown here.

Big and Small

Lizi and her doll, Kita, have their own sets of toys to play with.

Here are some big and small things.

The elephant is big.

The cat is small.

The towel is big.

The hanky is small.

The book is big.

The eraser is small.

The apple is big.

The cherries are small.

The pumpkin is big.

The potato is small.

The mouse is big.

The ant is small.

Observe that Kita has the smallest things.

It is lunch time! Draw strings to link the big things to Lizi and the small things to Kita.

It is time to dress up for school. Draw strings to join the big things to Lizi and the small things to Kita.

Sequencing

Look at the sets of objects given below. The biggest object in each is circled.

In each set, tick the biggest item.

Draw strings to match these things to the teddy bears based on their size.

One

RHYME

Straight line down, And then we're done.
That's the way to make one.

Trace the number.

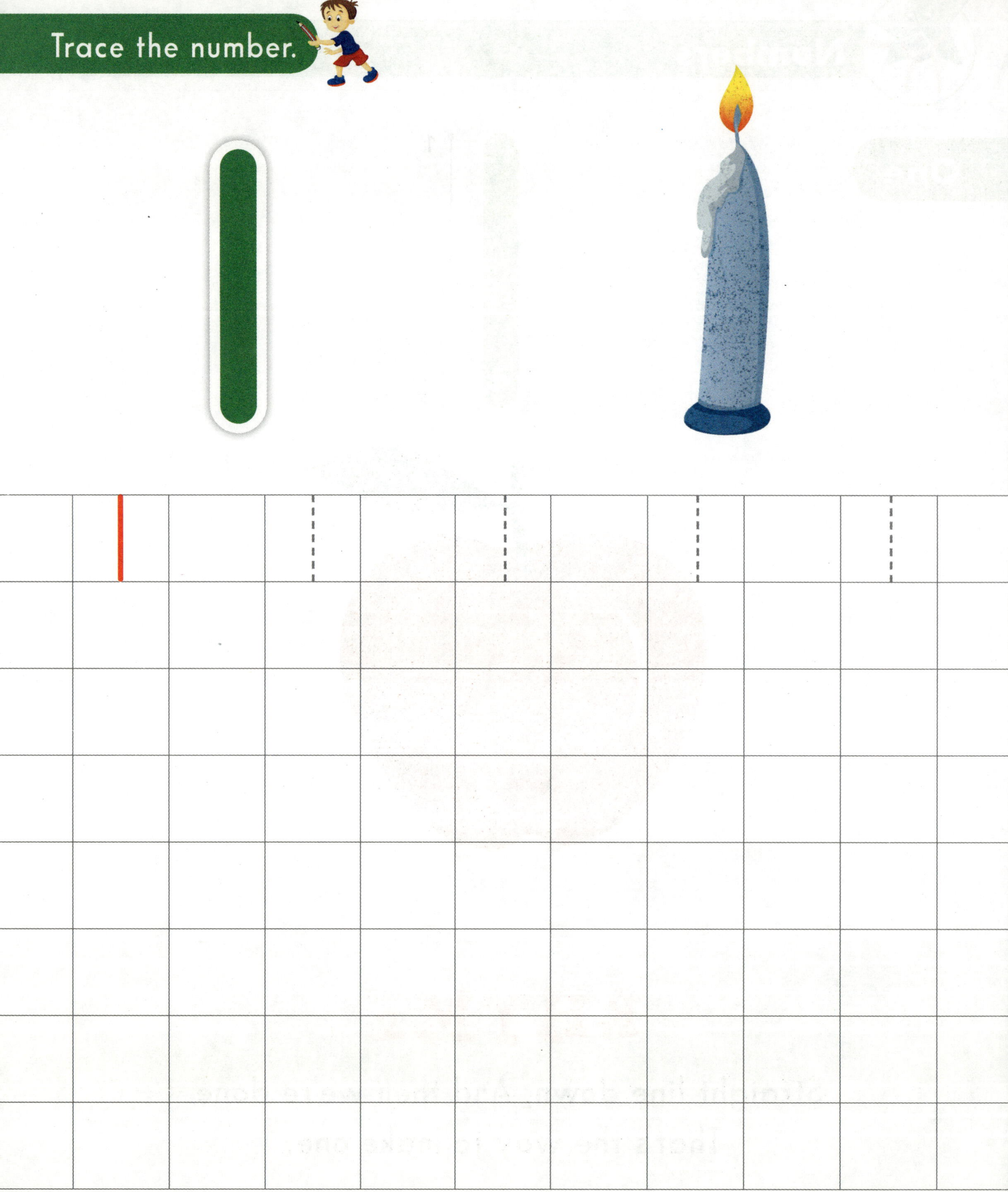

Look at the picture. How many of these things do you see?

Draw lines to match the things that are 1 in number to 1 in the centre.

Two

RHYME

Around and back, Then on the track.
Do doo, do doo, That's how we make two.

Look at the picture. Count the number of books on the table. How many pictures are hanging on the wall? How many table lamps are there?

Trace the number.

	2		2		2		2		2	

	2		2		2		2		2	

Draw lines to match the things that are 2 in number to 2 in the centre.

Count and write

Count the objects and write the number.

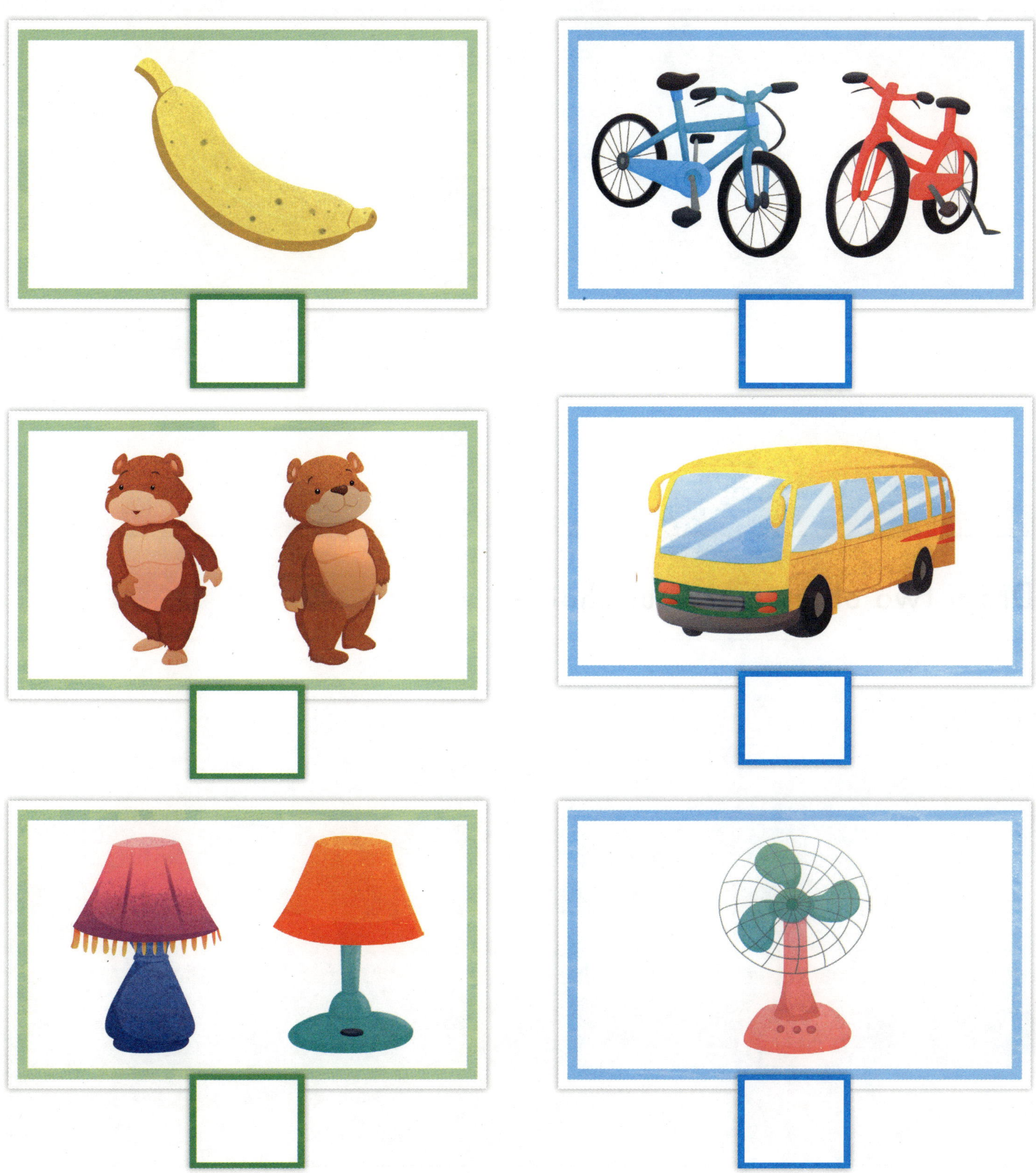

Let's draw

Draw one object of your choice.

Draw two objects of your choice.

Three

RHYME

Around a tree, Around a tree.
That's the way to make three.

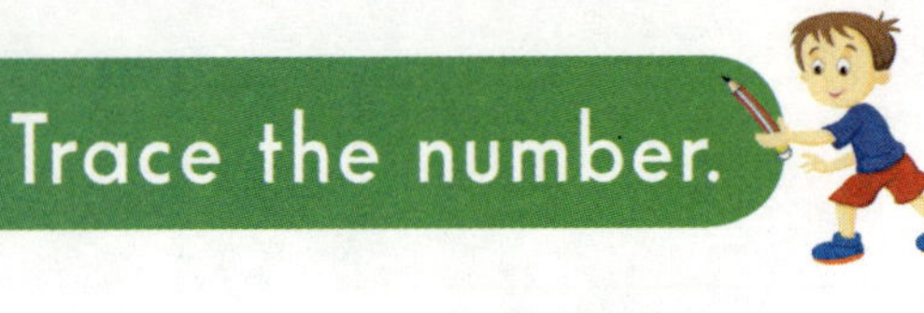

	3		3		3		3		3	

3 3 3 3 3

Draw lines to match the things that are 3 in number to 3 in the centre.

Four

RHYME

A standing line, A sleeping line,
A standing line once more,
That's how we make four.

Trace the number.

	4		4		4		4		4	

	4		4		4		4		4	

Look at the picture. How many birds are there?

Draw lines to match the things that are 4 in number to 4 in the centre.

Count and tell

Count the number of objects in each box and circle the correct number.

Let's draw

Draw four balls.

Draw one candle.

Draw two lollipops.

Draw three flowers.

Five

RHYME

Straight line down, Then around.
Hat on top, Five is a clown.

Trace the number.

5		5		5		5		5	

	5		5		5		5		5	

Draw lines to match the things that are 5 in number to 5 in the centre.

5

Count and write the number of objects.

Observe how the numbers are written in sequence on the number train.

Write the missing numbers in the number train.

Count and match

Draw lines to match the groups that have the same number of objects.

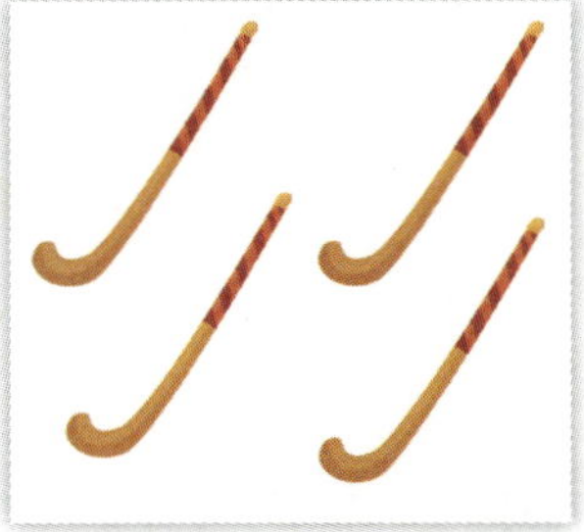

Join the dots

Join the dots from 1 to 5 to make carrots for the rabbit. Colour the carrots red.

Six

RHYME

A big curve that goes into its tummy.
We made six that sure looks funny!

Trace the number.

6 6 6 6 6

	6		6		6		6		6	

Find the way

Draw a line to help the rabbit reach the basket with six carrots.

Seven

RHYME

Across the sky and down from heaven.
That's the way to make seven.

Trace the number.

7	7	7	7	7

Ben wants to keep seven cookies in each tray. Each tray already has some cookies in it. Draw more to make seven in each.

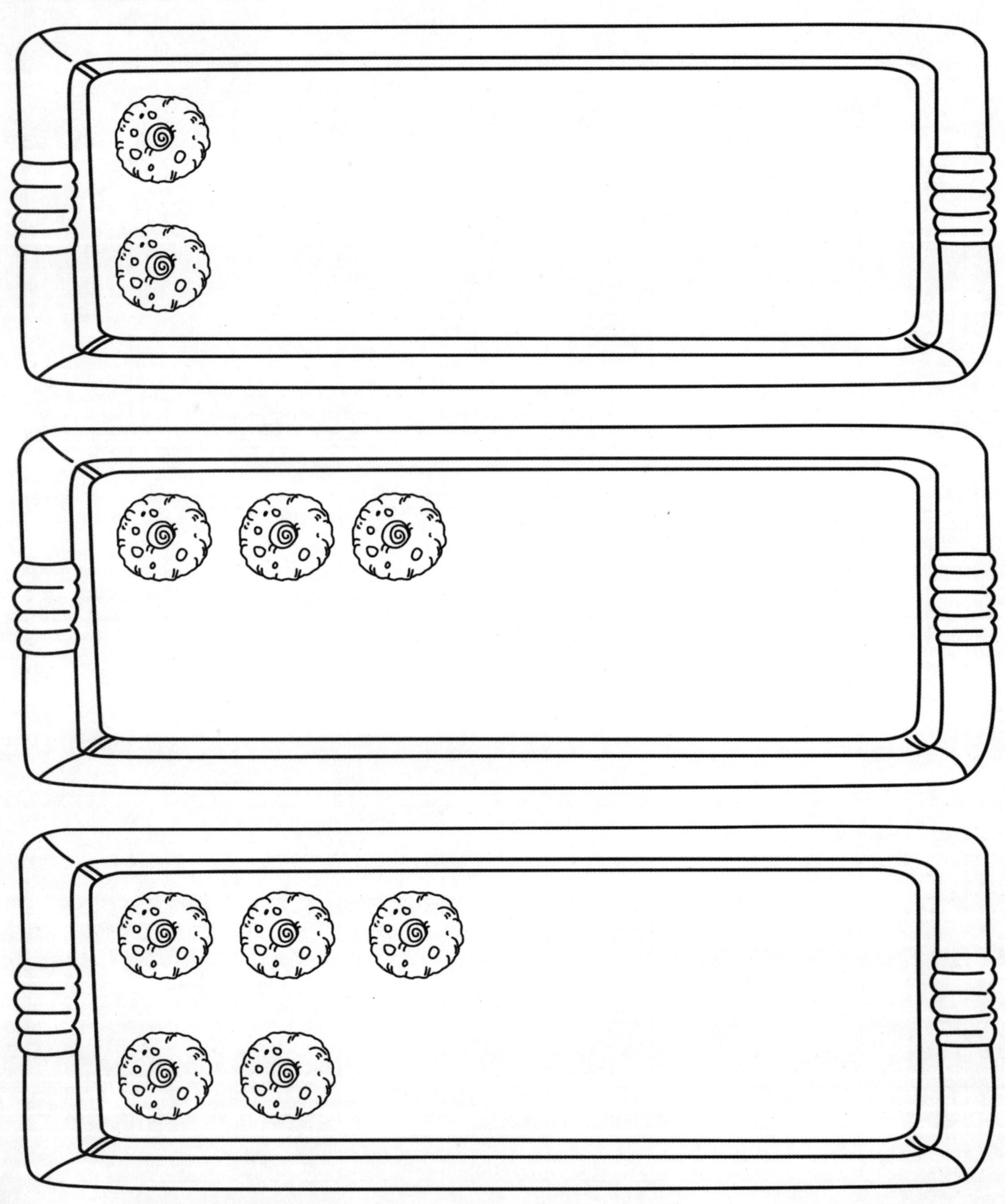

Count and match

Match the number of objects in each group to the numbers in the centre.

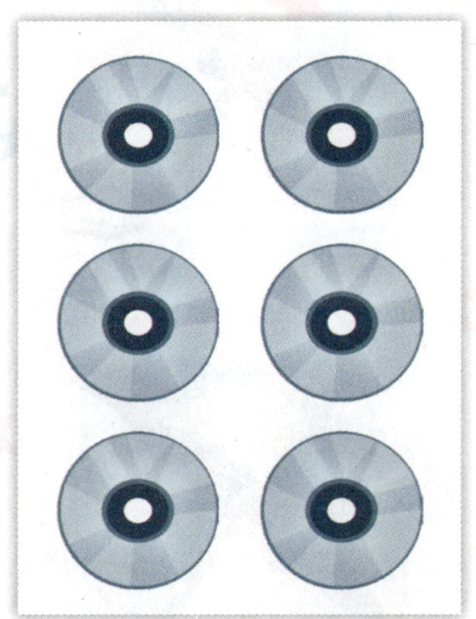

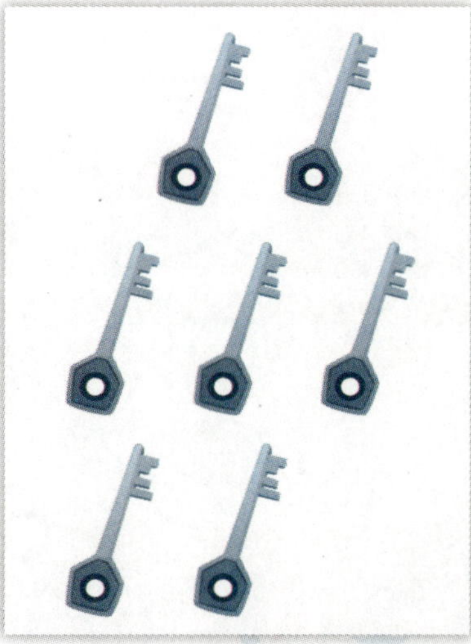

Eight

RHYME

Make an S and do not wait
Go back up and that's an eight.

Trace the number.

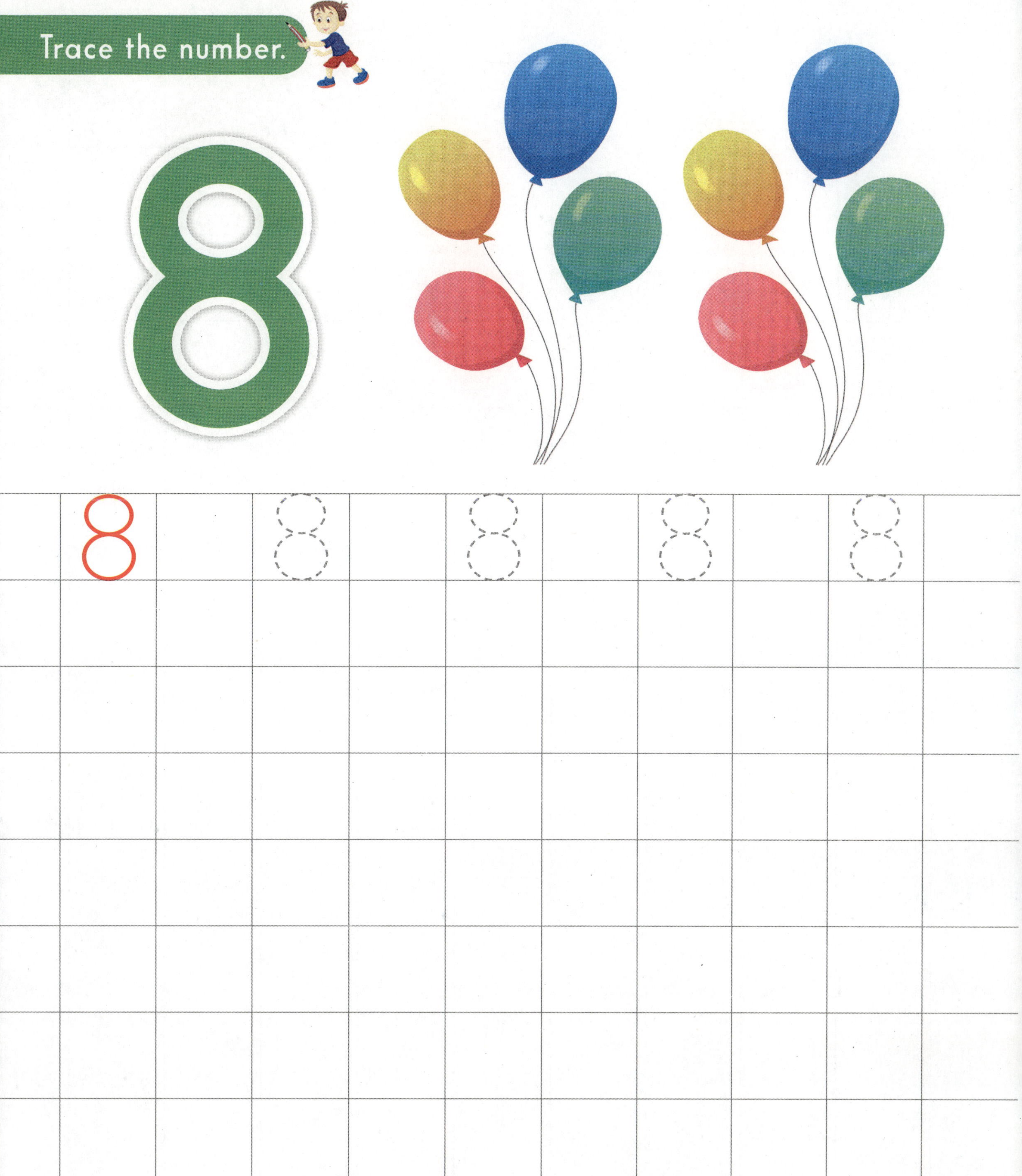

8 8 8 8 8

Lizi has a bunch of five flowers. Draw a bunch of eight flowers.

Join the dots to make eight and complete the picture.

Nine

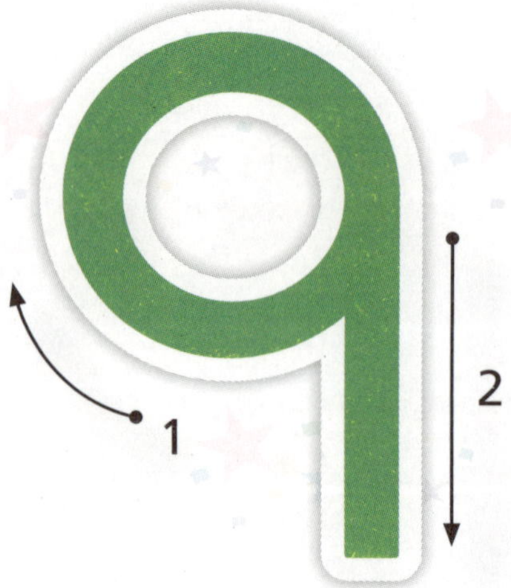

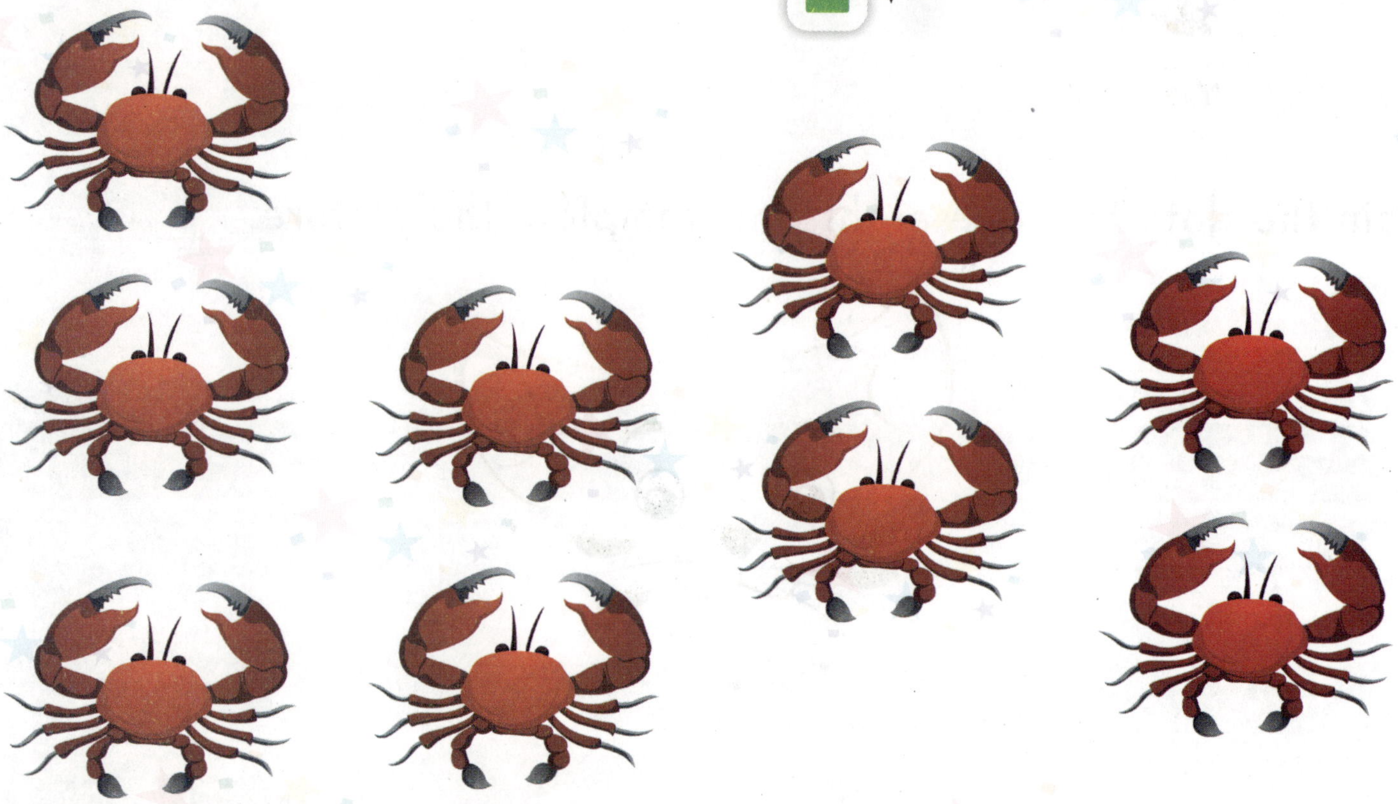

9

1

2

A loop and a line,
That makes number nine.

Trace the number.

	9		9		9		9		9	

Count and match

Match the number of objects in each group to the numbers in the centre.

More and less

Ben went to the zoo. He took some bananas to feed the monkeys. He gave one banana to each monkey. Give one banana to each monkey.

After giving one banana to each monkey, he still had a banana with him. So, the bananas were more and the monkeys were less.

Count the objects in each group and then tick the one that has more objects.

Count the objects in each group and then tick the one that has more objects.

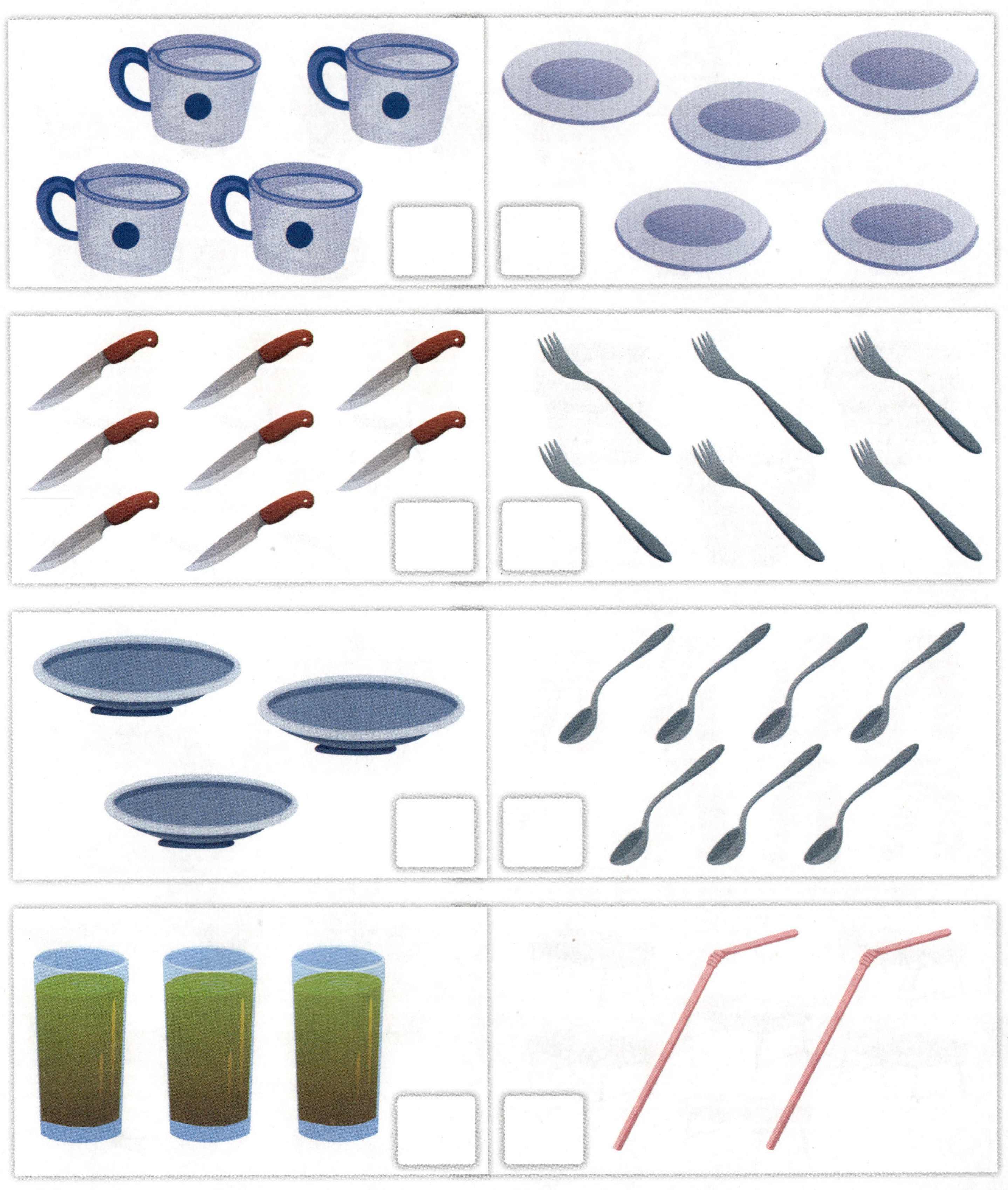

Count the objects in each group and then tick the one that has less objects.

Let's draw more

Draw more objects in the second tray than given in the first tray.

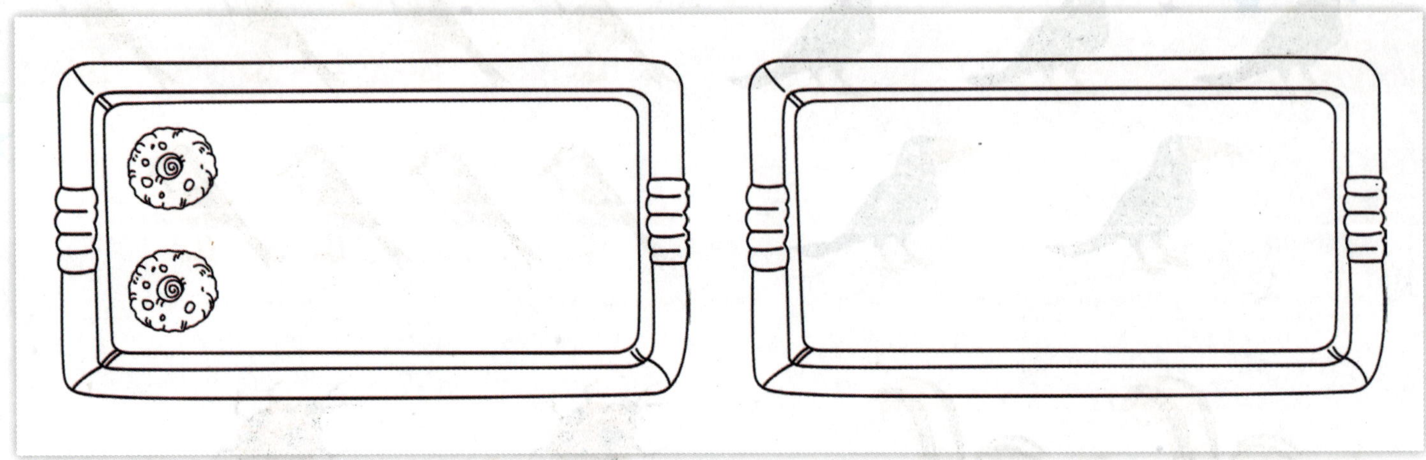

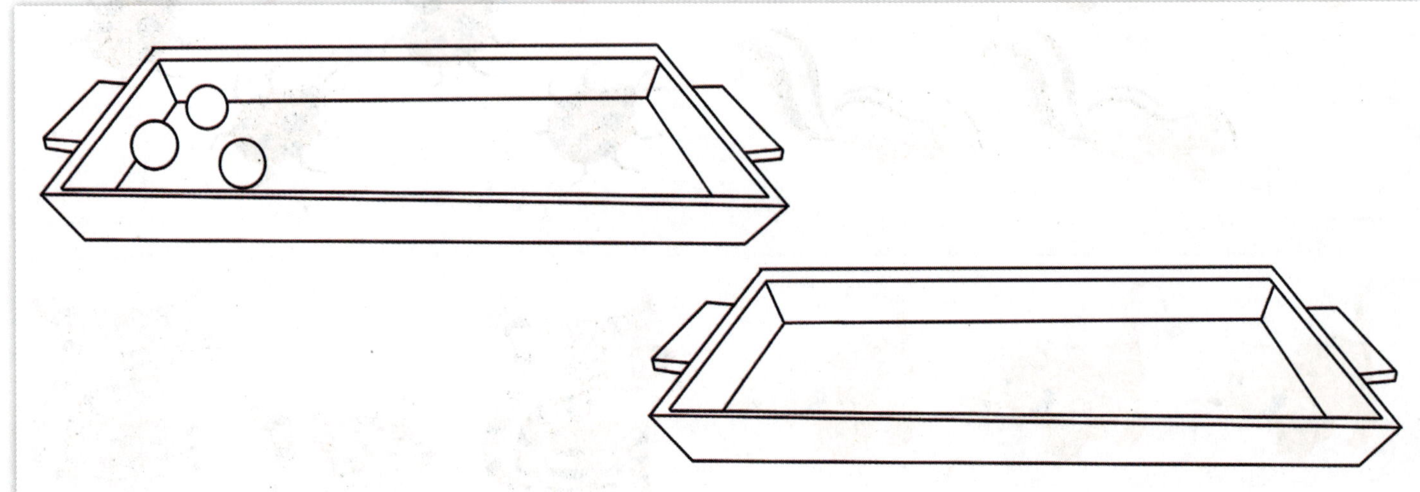

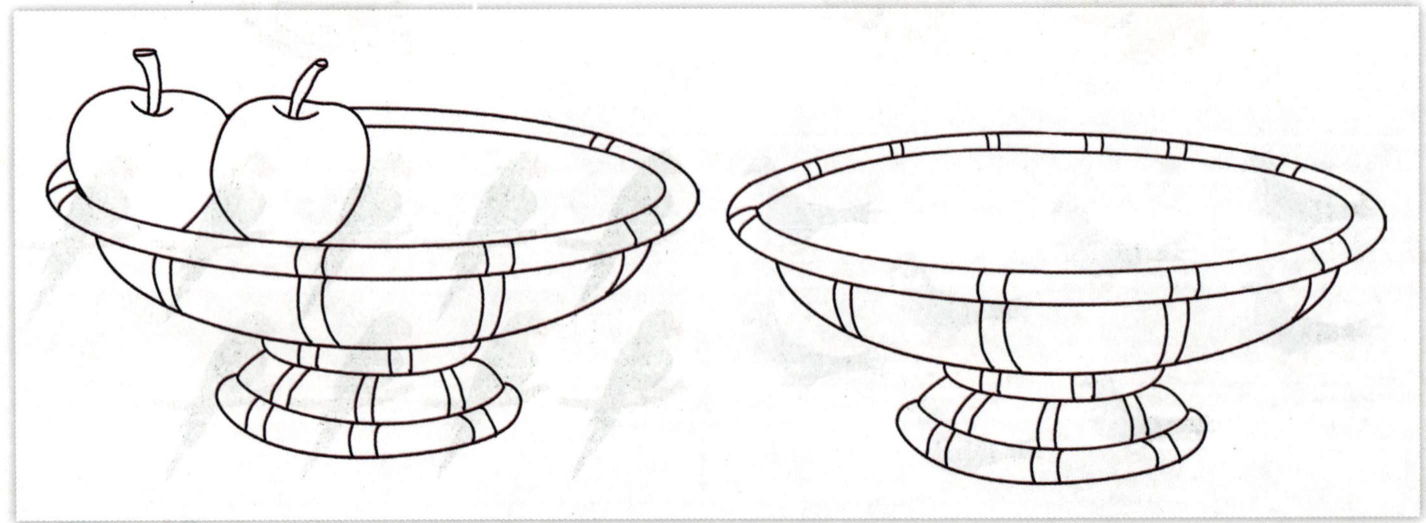

Look at the icons. Count the number of these things in the scene and write it in the box.

Fill in the missing numbers.

Count and colour

Colour the boxes according to the number given.

1	2	3	4	5	6	7	8	9

Zero

Ben was counting the number of beads in each string.

He saw a string with no bead. He did not know which number meant nothing. His mother told him that 0 (zero) is the number that stands for nothing. Then she asked him to write the number of biscuits in each jar. Can you help Ben in counting the biscuits in the jar?

The story of zero

One day a teacher invited all the numbers from 0 to 9 to a party. All the numbers started teasing 0. Number 1 told 0, 'My value is 1, but you have no value.' The other numbers also teased 0 saying that it has no value. 0 felt very sad and began to cry. Then the teacher called all the numbers and told them that 0 is valuable, too. She called Number 1 and made 0 stand next to him. Now, 1 became 10.

She told all the numbers that they too can increase their value by being friends with 0. The numbers promised not to make fun of 0 and made 0 their friend.

Ten

RHYME

One and zero, They become friends.
That's how we get number ten.

Ben is walking home from the park. Count the number of stones he has to walk on to reach home. Number the stones in the right order.

Trace the number.

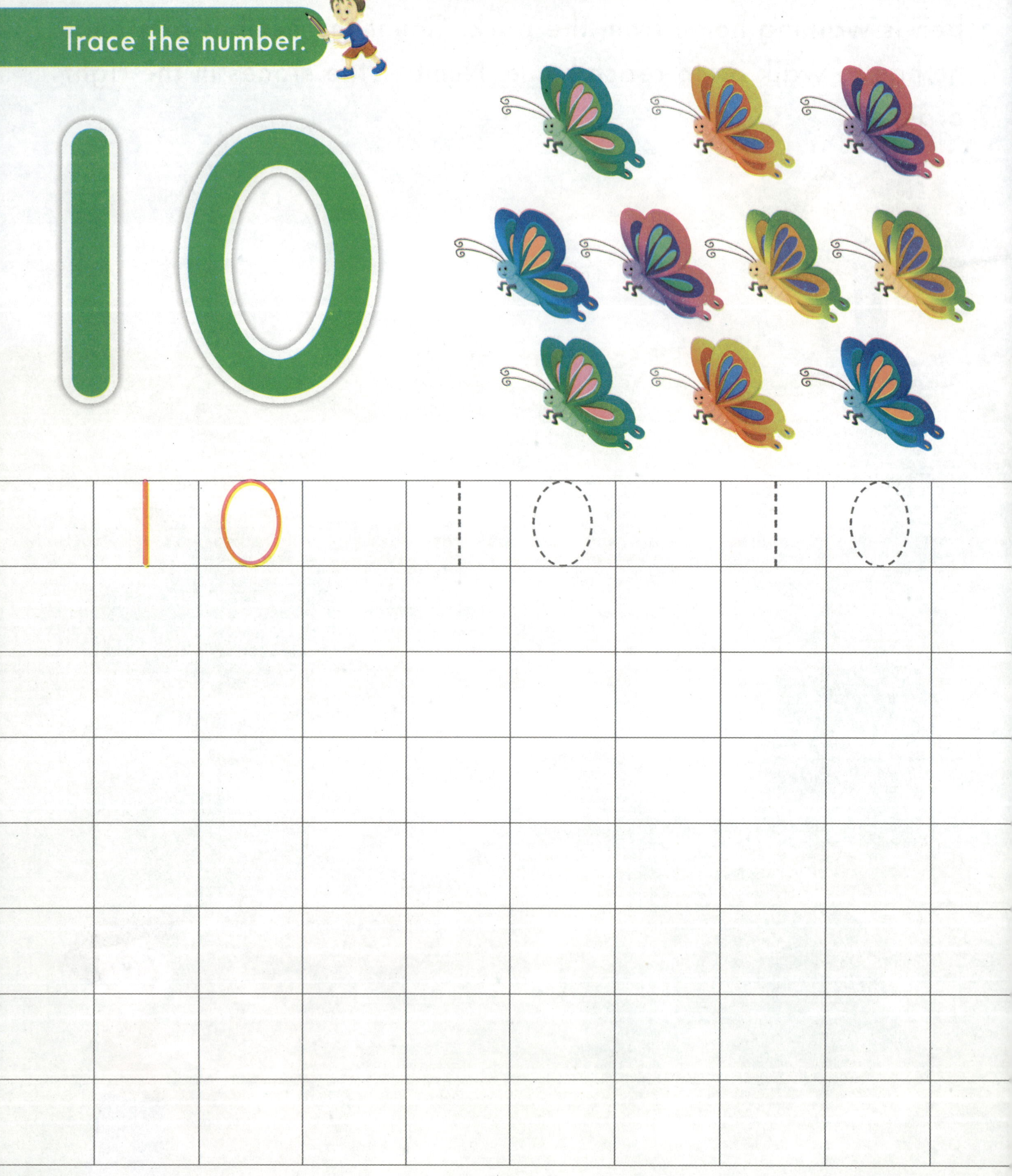

10 10 10

Let's draw

Draw balls according to the given number.

6

7

10

9

8

Ben is holding ten balloons in his hand. Number the balloons from 1 to 10.

Inside and Outside

Lizi and Kita are inside the house.

Lizi and Kita go outside the house for a walk.

They come back and Kita sits in her basket.

Kita comes out of the basket to drink milk.

Ice in the glass
Ice outside the glass

Flower in the vase
Flower outside the vase

Goldfish inside the jar
Goldfish outside the jar

Pencils inside the holder
Pencil outside the holder

Boy in the pool
Boy outside the pool

Book inside the bag
Book outside the bag

Look at the pictures and tick the animal that is inside.

Look at the picture. Tick the fruits that are outside the basket.

Near and Far

Near

Far

Near

Far

Observe the picture carefully and tick the right answer.

1. What is near the tree? 🏠 / 🚗
2. What is far from the tree? 🏠 / 🚗
3. What is near the house? 🌳 / 🚗
4. What is far from the house? 🌳 / 🚗

Tick the right option.

What is far from the tree?

What is near the tree?

Who is near the tree?

Let's draw

Draw two stars near the moon. Use a sketch pen.

Draw two kites far from the sun. Use a sketch pen.

Subitizing

Look at the dot cards. The skill of reading without actually counting is called subitizing. It helps to speed up calculations.

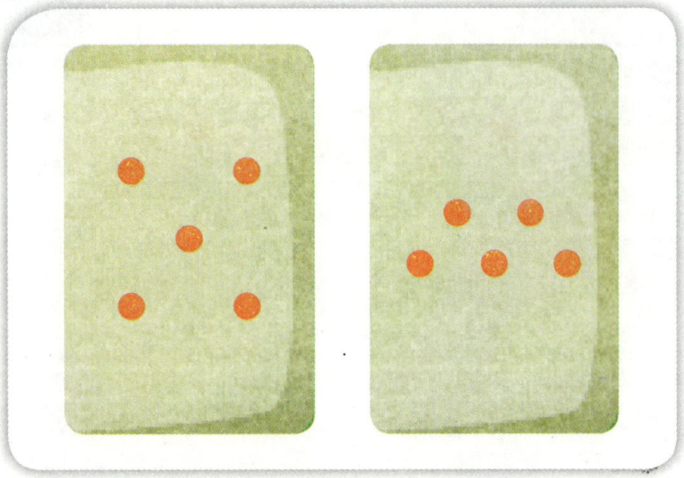

Look at the dot cards. Match the dot cards which represent the same number. Do not count but use the skill of subitizing.

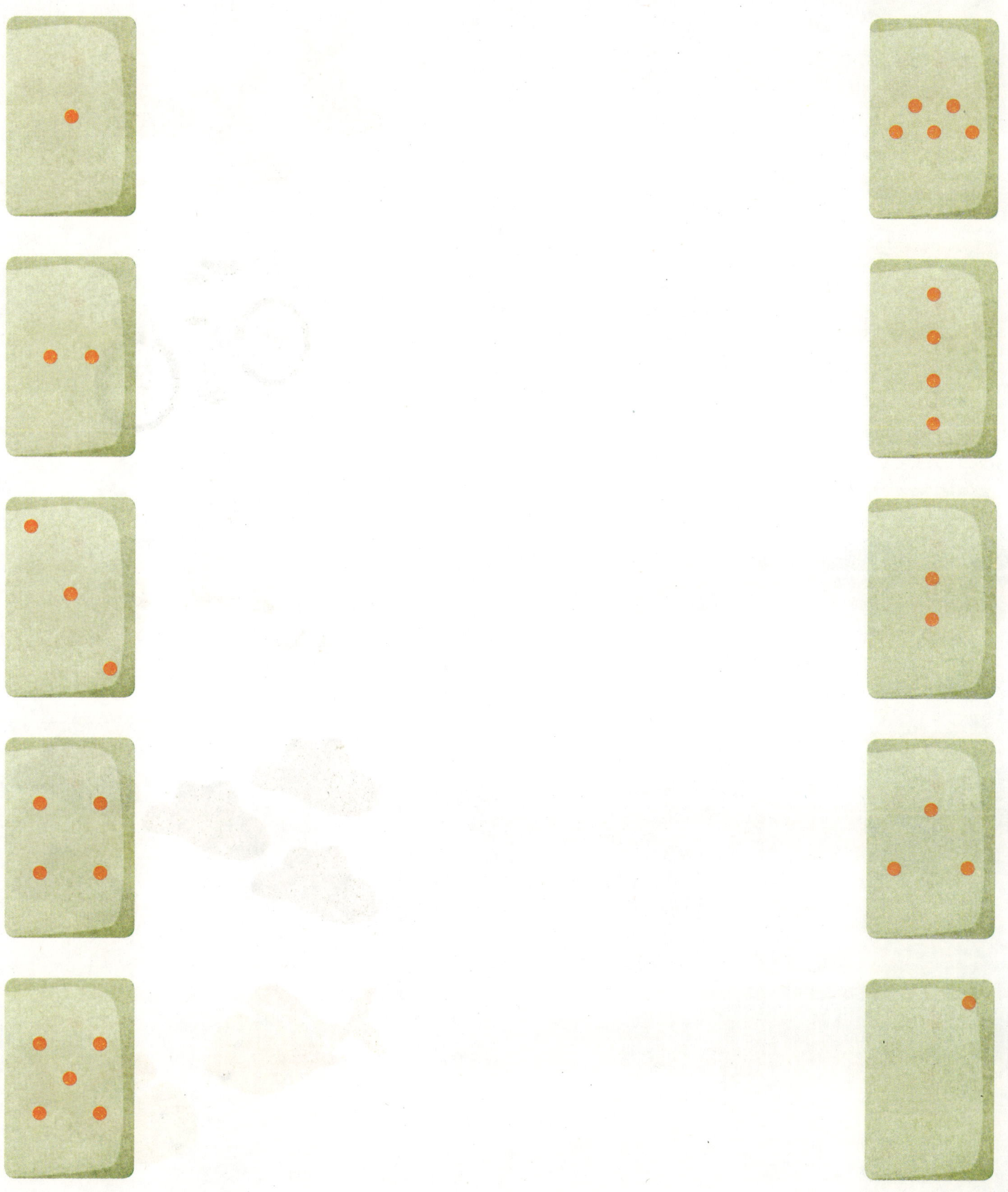

Match the dot cards to the group they represent.

Shapes

Circle

Circle

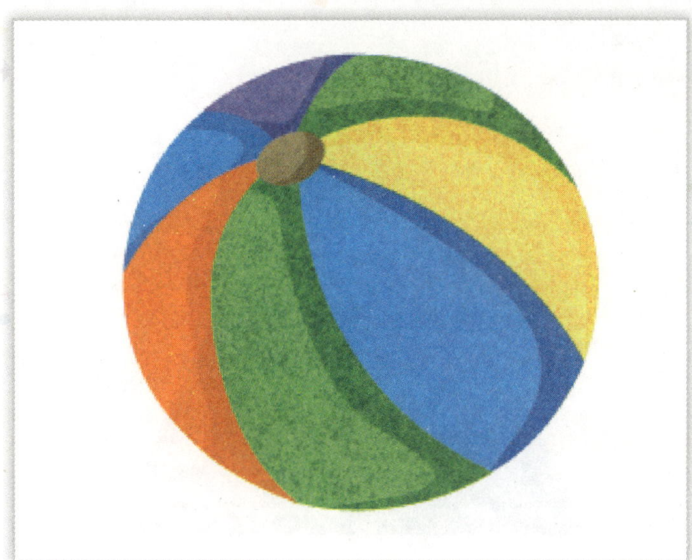

Ball

Sun

Doughnut

Bangle

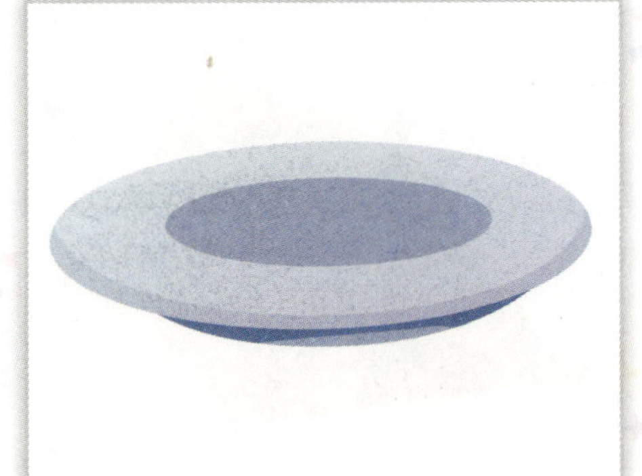

Plate

Ring

Wheel

Triangle

Triangle

Christmas tree

Pizza

Cheese

Sandwich

Sail

Flag

Tent

Square

Square

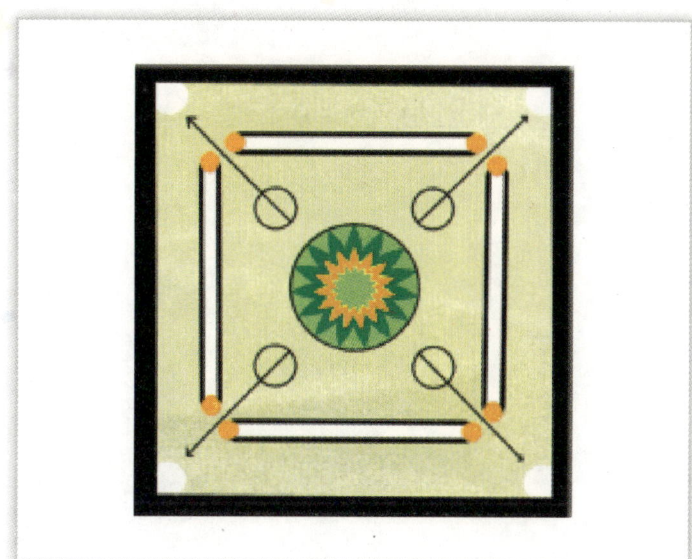

Carrom board

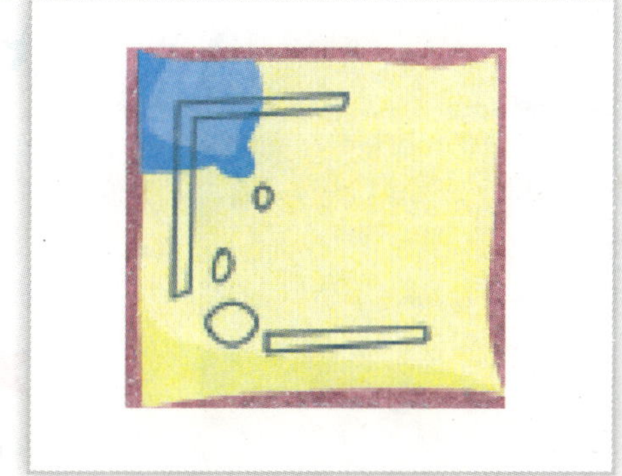

Handkerchief

Painting

Chessboard

Ludo

Cushion

Bread

Rectangle

Rectangle

Door

Table

Book

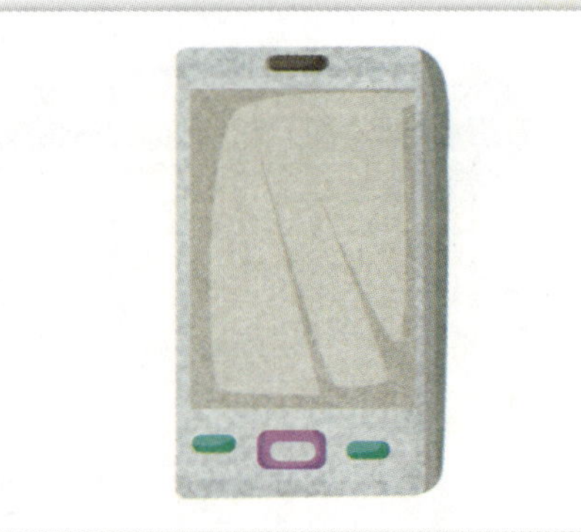

Mobile

Brick

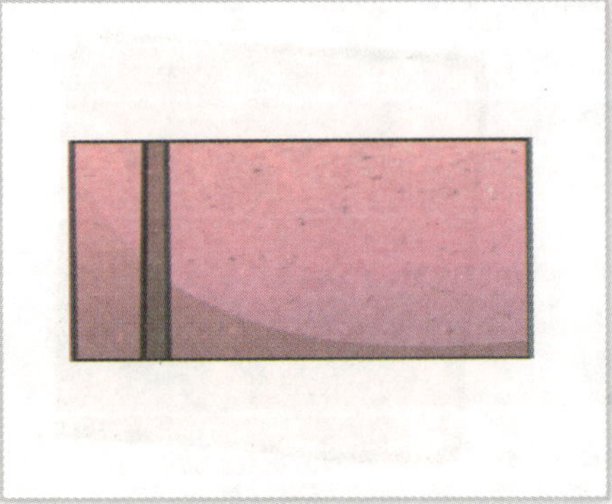

Doormat

Photo frame

Observe the picture. Tick all the things that have the shape of a circle.

Let's draw circles

Paste/draw pictures of any four objects that have the shape of a circle.

Observe the picture. Tick all the things that have the shape of a triangle.

Let's draw triangles

Paste/draw pictures of any four objects that have the shape of a triangle.

Observe the picture. Tick all the things that have the shape of a square.

Paste/draw pictures of any four objects that have the shape of a square.

Observe the picture. Tick all the things that have the shape of a rectangle.

Paste/draw pictures of any four objects that have the shape of a rectangle.

Find the following shapes in the picture and write their number.

Patterns

Lizi has arranged her books on the shelf. Observe how she has done it. Is there any repetition?

Yes! You are right! Blue-red-blue-red and so on.

Look how her mother has arranged the vegetables.

Look how Kita's toys are arranged.

Lizi is making a birthday card for her friend. Observe how she is making a pattern on the card.

Look at the bedsheet and observe the pattern.

Look at the towel. What a beautiful pattern!

Now we can create our own patterns.

Observe the patterns and tick the one that should come next.

Lizi and her friends are making cards. Observe the pattern and continue.

|O|O|O|O|O|O _ _ _ _ _ _

|-|-|-|-|-|-|- _ _ _ _ _ _

△○△○△○△ _ _ _ _ _ _

+÷+÷+÷+÷ _ _ _ _ _ _

X-X-X-X-X-X-X- _ _ _ _ _ _

□○□○□○□ _ _ _ _ _ _

Heavy and Light

Ben wants to rearrange his room. He wants to change the place of the sofa. He easily picks up the cushions. They are light.

He tries to move the sofa but cannot; the sofa is heavy.

He wants to move the computer table; it is heavy. Then he picks up the CDs; they are light.

He wants to move the centre table; it is too heavy. He picks up the flower vase; it is light.

Ben went to the playground. He placed some objects on the see-saw. The side with the heavy object went down.

He placed a big stone on one side and a feather on the other side. The big stone was heavy. The feather was light.

He placed a leaf on one side and his bag on the other side. The bag was heavy. The leaf was light.

He placed a mango on one side and a flower on the other side. The mango was heavy. The flower was light.

Tick the heavier object.

Tick the lighter object.

Long and Short

Lizi and her mother were reading a picture book. Lizi showed her mother that both the cow and the goat had a tail.

Her mother told her to notice that the tail of the cow was long and the tail of the goat was short.

Lizi told her mother, 'Your hair is long and my hair is short!'

Her mother showed her more things which were long and short.

Tick the long object. Cross the short one.

Draw the tail of these animals. The tail of the monkey should be long. The tail of the rabbit should be short.

Draw a long pencil and a short pencil. Colour the short pencil.

Time

Ben gets up early in the morning.

He brushes his teeth.

He takes a bath.

He goes to school.

He plays in the evening.

He reads storybooks at night.

He sleeps.

Look at the sequence and observe the order in which these people are doing their tasks.

Look at these activities. Draw a sun ☀ if these are done during the day or a star ★ if they are done at night.

Write 1, 2 or 3 in the boxes according to the sequence in which the following activities are done.

Up and Down

Up

Down

Observe the scene. Some things are up in the sky and some things are down on the ground.

Here are some things from the scene on the previous page. Colour the circle blue for the things in the sky and green for the things on the ground.

In each picture, tick the frog that is up.

In each picture, tick the ant that is down.

Data Collection

Ben is going to his uncle's shop. In the evening, he wants to bring chocolate cookies and almond cookies for his father, mother and sister. He wants to know how many cookies of each type to bring. So he asks them which cookie they like and puts a smiley for each.

Family	Chocolate cookie	Almond cookies
Total	2	2

So now he knows that he has to bring 2 and 2 cookies.

Ben is very happy. His mother asked him to join the numbers from 1-10 on this sheet. What did he get?

Join the dots from 1-10 to complete the picture.

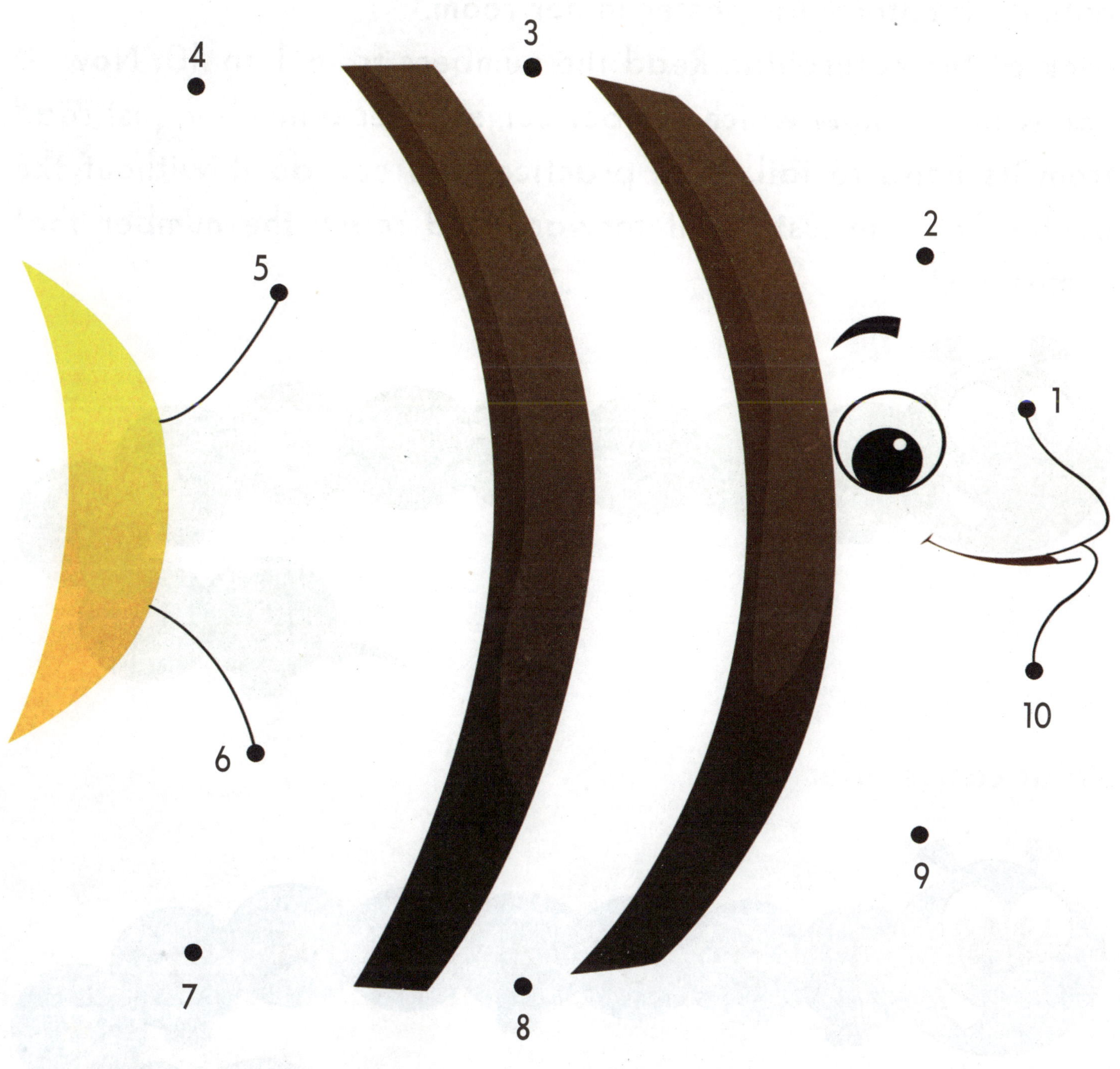

What comes after?

Lizi asks her mother which number comes after 5? Her mother puts up a caterpillar poster in her room.

Look at the caterpillar. Read the numbers from 1 to 10. Now, if you want to know which number comes after a number, just read from its head to tail. With practice, you can do it without the poster. You can just count forward and reach the number that comes next.

What comes after 8?

What comes before?

Lizi asks her mother which number comes before 5? Her mother again tells her to look at the caterpillar poster in her room. Read the numbers from 1 to 10. Now, if you want to know which number comes before a number, just read from its tail to head. With practice, you can do it without the poster. You can just count backwards and reach the number that comes before.

What comes before 8?

What comes between?

Lizi asks her mother which number comes between 4 and 6? Her mother tells her to look at the caterpillar poster in her room. Read the numbers from 1 to 10.

Now, if you want to know which number comes between two numbers, just find the two numbers and read the number between them. With practice, you can do it without the poster. You can just count and find out. What comes between 4 and 6?

What comes between 7 and 9?

What comes after the given number?

2 ____ 4 ____ 1 ____

3 ____ 7 ____ 9 ____

What comes before the given number?

____ 9 ____ 7 ____ 5

____ 3 ____ 2 ____ 8

What comes between the given numbers?

2 ____ 4 5 ____ 7

8 ____ 10 4 ____ 6

7 ____ 9 1 ____ 3

Write 1 to 10.

1									
2									
3									
4									
5									

6

7

8

9

10

Activity

Fill the missing numbers.

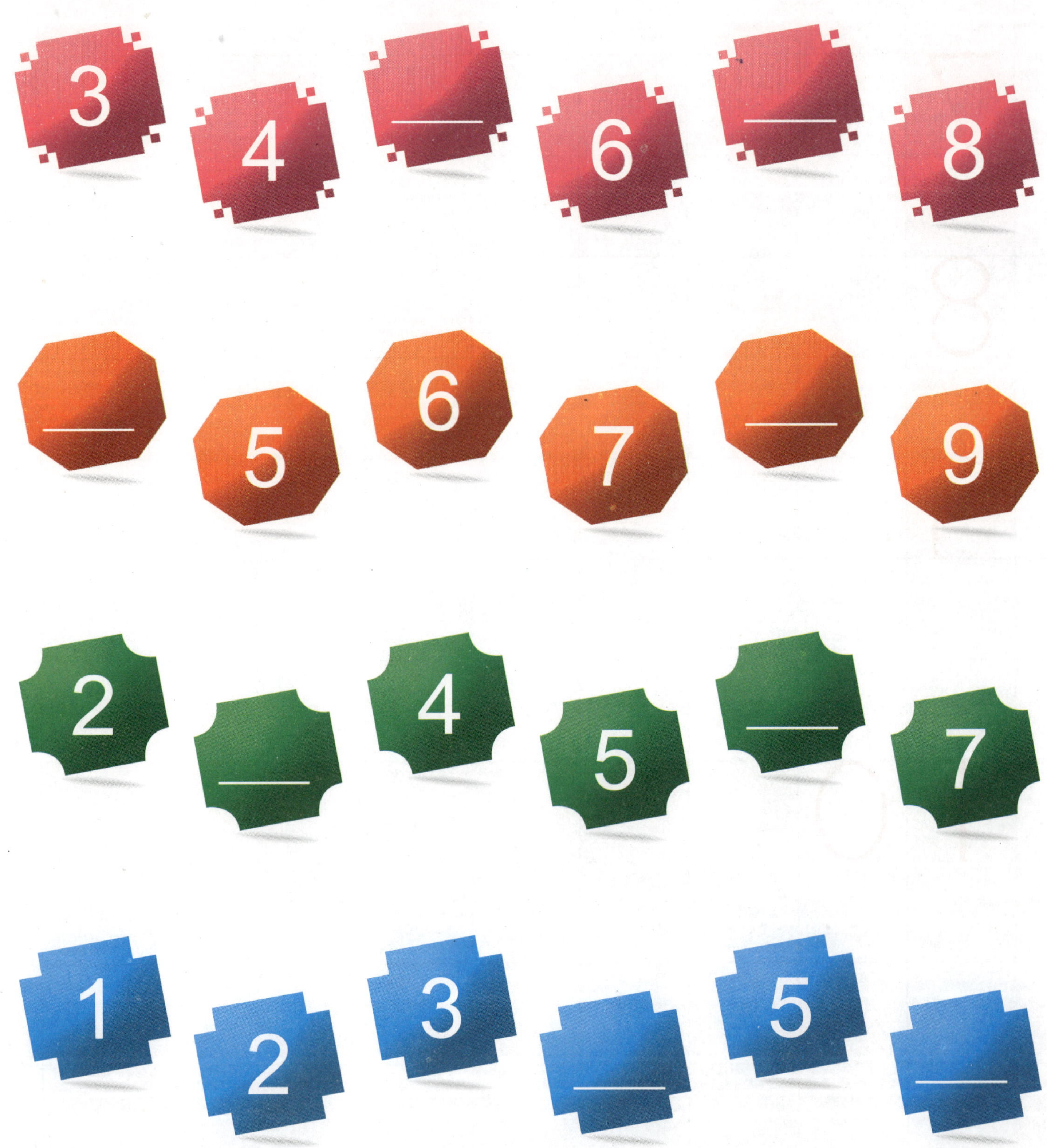